Colourful Creatures

Nicolas Brasch

Contents

Meet Tessa

Hi, I'm Tessa. I take photos of animals. I like colourful animals the most!

An animal's colour can help it do different things. Come on – I'll show you!

Don’t Eat Me!

Some animals use colour to stop other animals eating them.

common tiger butterfly

Tiger Butterfly

Birds eat butterflies, but they don't eat the tiger butterfly! Its black and orange colour tells birds to stay away. Birds think that it will taste really bad!

Just Like Me!

This butterfly looks just like the tiger butterfly. Its black and orange colour tells birds to stay away. Birds think it will taste bad, too – just like the tiger butterfly.

leopard lacewing butterfly

common tiger butterfly

Can you spot the difference?

A Tricky Hunter

Some animals use colour to trick other animals.

Tiger

The tiger has orange fur with black stripes.

The tiger uses **camouflage** (say: *cam-oh-flarj*) to help it hunt. Its colour helps it hide in long grass. Other animals can't see it coming!

I'm Watching You!

Tigers have white spots on the backs of their ears. These spots look like eyes. They are called '**eye-spots**'!

When a tiger is young, eye-spots help to keep it safe. The spots trick other animals into thinking the tiger is looking at it!

Eye-spots

Some butterflies have eye-spots to scare away other animals, too. It looks as if this butterfly has eyes on its wings!

Look at Me!

Many animals use colour to find a **mate**.

Peacocks

Peacocks have bright colours on their tails. Their tail feathers are blue and green. The feathers have spots that look like eyes.

Male and Female

Males are called peacocks.
Females are called peahens.

Only peacocks have bright coloured tails. Peahens are brown.

When a peacock sees a peahen, he opens up his tail feathers. This makes the peahen look at him and his colourful tail.

Colourful Changes

Some animals can change colour!

Cuttlefish

Cuttlefish live in the sea.
They can change colour to hide.
They use their colour as camouflage.

Cuttlefish can change to the colour of what is around them.

This cuttlefish is brown and white, like the sand around it.

This cuttlefish is red, like the rocks around it.

Chameleon

The chameleon (say: *ca-meel-i-an*) is a type of lizard.

There are lots of different kinds of chameleon. Most of them can change colour. Different chameleons can change into different colours. These can be:

- pink
- green
- blue
- red
- black
- yellow!

Chameleons change colour to camouflage themselves. They change colour to find mates, too. A male chameleon will show a bright colour to find a female.

A Colour Battle!

Male chameleons sometimes have a colour battle! The winner is the one with the brightest colour.

More Colourful Creatures

How do these animals use colour?

Glossary

camouflage
colours that help animals hide from other animals

eye-spots
coloured spots on an animal that look a bit like eyes

mate
an animal to make a baby with

Index

Quiz Answers
1. To find a mate
2. As camouflage to trick other animals
3. To tell other animals to keep away